Kids' COOKBOOK

Tantalisingly tasty lunch box ideas
for junior chefs

GINA STEER

SELECT
EDITIONS

A QUANTUM BOOK

Paperback edition published by
Selectabook Ltd.
Selectabook Distribution Centre,
Folly Road,
Roundway,
Devizes
Wiltshire SN10 2HT

ISBN 1-86160-480-7

This book is produced by
Quantum Publishing Ltd.
6 Blundell Street
London N7 9BH

QUMKLB

Printed in Hong Kong by
Sing Cheong Printing Co. Ltd.

ACKNOWLEGEMENTS

Special thanks to Spencer and Victoria Dewing,
Tom Lolobo, Gee Hyun Kim, Nick Seruwagi,
James and Lucy Stuart and to Bob McNiff of the
Burlington Junior School, New Malden, Surrey.

Publisher's Note

Children should take great care when cooking.
Certain techniques such as slicing and chopping
or using the stove, oven or grill can be
dangerous and extreme care must be exercised
at all times. Adults should always supervise
while children work in the kitchen.
As far as methods and techniques mentioned in
this book are concerned, all statements,
information and advice given here are believed
to be true and accurate. However, the author,
copyright holder, nor the publisher can accept
any legal liability for errors or omissions.

Contents

1

A POCKET FULL OF GOODNESS

2

PICK A STICK

3

OPEN TOPPERS

4

SANDWICHES TO GO

5

MOUTHWATERING SALADS

6

CRUNCHY BITES

7

SWEET DELIGHTS

Introduction

As long as you can read you can cook, and you're never too young to start. Cooking is fun and it is a great feeling when you eat something you have cooked yourself. When it tastes good and your family and friends enjoy it as well, then it is really satisfying.

The recipes in this book are easy to follow, with clear step-by-step pictures showing the different techniques required. Some of the photographs are bordered in red, and the instructions are highlighted in **bold text** for safety reasons. You should ensure that there is an adult present as these steps involve using either sharp knives, hot liquids or utensils which you could easily harm yourself with.

When cooking, whatever age you are, there are a few basic rules to follow so you do not hurt yourself or have a disaster in the kitchen. Providing you follow these, you will find that cooking will give you hours of fun as well as many tasty treats to enjoy.

Read the next few pages first before you start to cook. Then just put your apron on and begin.

Happy Cooking

Before You Begin

▌ One of the most important rules when cooking is to read the recipe right through before you start to do anything. For some recipes, ingredients are soaked overnight or the dish needs to be chilled for a long period and this would be no good if you wanted the dish the same day you started making it.

▌ Check that you have everything you need to make a recipe. Discovering half way through that you need to pop down to the shops to buy one of the ingredients spoils the fun.

▌ When you start to cook, begin with the easy recipes and once you have mastered these, then move on to those that are a little more complicated.

Hygiene

▌ Hygiene is very important when handling and preparing food as germs can very easily be passed on through bad habits. Ensure that everything you use is kept as clean as possible, especially your hands.

▌ If you have cuts or sores on your hands, cover them with a clean plaster.

▌ NEVER use the same chopping boards, knives, etc. to prepare both raw and cooked food, either use clean ones or wash them in between.

▌ Do not play with your pets while cooking and keep them off the work surfaces at all times, especially when food is being prepared.

▌ Make sure that the work surfaces are clean before you start to cook and always use clean tea towels and dish clothes.

▌ Check that all the implements you are going to use are clean before using them. If not, wash them in hot water as often as possible and rinse all the soapy bubbles off. It is better to use rubber gloves to protect your hands so you can use hotter water.

▌ With left-over food or hot food that is to be kept, cool as quickly as possible then place, lightly covered in the refrigerator. Do not leave it sitting on the side for ages as this is how germs breed and multiply.

▌ Wash all fresh foods such as fruit, vegetables and salad ingredients before using in the recipe or eating.

▌ Every cook enjoys tasting their food while they are cooking, but do not dip and lick, use a clean spoon when you want to taste and wash it after use every time.

First Steps

▌ Put your apron on, tie your hair back, and wash your hands.

▌ Read the recipe through and assemble all the ingredients and implements you need.

▌ Check that it is alright to use the kitchen and that there will be an adult around when you get to the steps that are highlighted.

▌ If, after reading the recipe, you are not sure about a step, ask first so that you understand.

▌ Measure your ingredients accurately.

▌ Try not to make too much mess as this makes cooking harder. Also do not just walk away when you have finished. Clean up afterwards, washing up and putting everything away.

Some Cookery Techniques

CHOPPING ONIONS

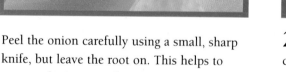

Peel the onion carefully using a small, sharp knife, but leave the root on. This helps to prevent the juices making you cry.

1 Hold the onion with one hand, with the root resting on the chopping board. Keep your fingers clear, and cut thin slices from the top almost to the root at the bottom.

2 Turn the onion round in a half circle then cut again from the top almost to the root.

3 Now place the onion on its side and cut 5mm slices.

4 Continue until you get to the root.

GRATING

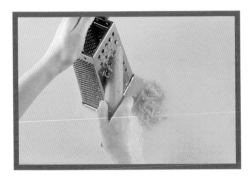 

Place the grater on a chopping board. Peel the vegetable if necessary, then holding the handle of the grater firmly with one hand, rub the vegetable *down* the grater, not up *and* down. Normally, you need to use the side of the grater that has the largest holes. This is known as grating coarsely. Watch your fingers as you get towards the end of the vegetable.

An easy way to grate lemon, orange or lime rind is to use the side of the grater that has the medium sized holes. Rinse and dry the fruit then, holding the grater with one hand, rub the fruit down the side of the grater.

By far the best method of removing the rind that sticks on the grater, is to brush it off with a pastry brush.

CHOPPING AND SLICING

Chopping herbs Rinse the herbs and pat dry with absorbent kitchen paper. Cut or break off the stalks then place the leaves in a cup. Using a pair of scissors, snip the herbs until chopped. Use as soon as possible.

Slicing Remember to use a chopping board when slicing or cutting meat, vegetables etc. and make sure that there is an adult present. It is a good idea to keep a separate chopping

board for meat, fish, vegetables or fruit if you can. If you cannot, then do not forget to wash the board, knife and your hands in between. Place the food to be cut on a clean chopping board. Then, holding the food firmly with one hand take a small, sharp knife and cut. Make the cuts away from you and make sure you move away the hand which is holding the food after you have cut a few slices so that you do not end up cutting your hand.

EGGS

Cracking eggs Place a small bowl on the work surface then crack the egg on the side of the bowl. Gently place your thumbs into the crack in the shell and put your forefingers at the top of the egg. Gently pull them apart so that the egg slips into the bowl. Discard the shells.

Separating eggs To separate the yolk from the white, crack the egg but instead of letting the whole egg slip into the bowl, tilt the egg to one side so that the white can flow into the bowl and the yolk can stay in one side of the split shell. Once the shell is in two halves put the yolk into the other half of the shell so all the white can flow into the bowl.

Whisking Egg whites are often whisked so that air is incorporated into a recipe so that it rises during cooking, or is lighter. Place the egg whites in a clean mixing bowl, ensuring that there is no egg yolk with the white (they will not whisk if there is any yolk present). Stand the bowl on a damp cloth to prevent it from slipping or moving around. With a whisk, whip the egg whites until they are white and stiff. A good test is to turn the bowl upside down for a few seconds when you think they are ready. If the whites are stiff they will not move. Be careful though. Only tip them gently at first. If they move, they are not whisked enough and you need to beat them a bit more.

Creaming Beat butter and sugar together in a mixing bowl using a wooden spoon until the sugar has been completely mixed into the butter. The mixture needs to be light and fluffy.

Whipping Double or whipping cream is often whipped before being used. To do this, place the cream in a clean bowl, then place the bowl on a damp cloth and, using a whisk, whip the cream until thick. Take care not to over whip as the cream will curdle.

Cooking Tips

Chicken or turkey is cooked if, when pierced with a skewer in the thickest part of the bird (the thigh), the juices run clear, and the flesh is white. If juices or flesh are pink, it needs to cook for longer.

Vegetables are cooked if when pierced with a round bladed knife or fork they feel tender to the touch and the implement slides in and out easily. Don't forget however, that vegetables are better if eaten while still slightly crunchy.

Pasta can only really be tested by taste. Carefully remove a piece of pasta and when cool enough, taste. It should be soft but still retaining a bite or chewy texture. This is known as *al dente*.

Pasta is best cooked in plenty of boiling water. It is a good idea to add a few drops of oil as this will prevent the pasta sticking. As soon as the pasta is cooked, drain thoroughly and use immediately.

Rice is tested in the same way as pasta. It should also feel soft but with a slightly chewy texture or bite. Plain boiled rice is best if rinsed before cooking then added to double the amount of cold water. Bring to the boil and stir once, then cover the pan, lower the heat and simmer for 12–15 minutes or until cooked.

Cakes and biscuits are cooked when they have turned golden brown and feel firm to the touch when lightly pressed with a clean finger.

Pastry cases are baked "blind" so ensure that the pastry is cooked properly. To bake blind, either crumple up a sheet of tin foil and carefully place in the base of the lined pastry case, or, place a sheet of greaseproof paper in the base and cover with baking beans. Ceramic baking beans can be bought from cookware shops and can be used repeatedly, or you can use dried edible beans which can be used again but not as often. If the recipe calls for the pastry to be pricked with a fork, this is to ensure that the pastry does not rise during baking.

All quantities are given in both metric and imperial units but make sure that you stick to one system for each recipe as they are not interchangeable. A useful conversion chart for temperatures, weights and measures can be found on page 96.

Storage Tips

It is important that foods are correctly stored so they remain in good condition and safe to eat.

All fresh meat and poultry should be stored on a clean plate, towards the bottom of the refrigerator as soon as possible after buying it.

Fresh fish should also be placed on a clean plate and be loosely covered. Store towards the bottom of the refrigerator and eat within one day of purchase.

All frozen foods should be placed in the freezer as soon as possible after buying.

If you wish to freeze fresh food yourself, first turn the freezer to rapid freeze for at least one hour before you need to use it. Wrap the food to be frozen in freezer wrap or follow the instructions according to the recipe or on the packet and place in the fast freeze section. Leave until solid and thoroughly frozen before switching the freezer back to its normal setting.

Fresh green vegetables and salad ingredients should be stored in the salad compartment of the refrigerator and used, if possible, within two to three days. The longer they are kept the more they will spoil and their valuable mineral and vitamin content will be impaired.

Fresh fruit should be washed before eating and stored in a cool place. Soft fruits should be lightly rinsed and allowed to dry on absorbent kitchen paper just before eating, do not wash soft fruits then store them as they will spoil and become mushy.

Potatoes and most root vegetables should be taken out of any polythene wrapping and placed in a brown paper bag and stored in a cool dry place. Carrots will keep in the refrigerator a little longer than other root vegetables but keep them in a paper bag not polythene as they could sweat and become wet and slimy.

Eggs should be kept in the refrigerator as should all dairy products such as butter, milk and cheese. Cheese is better if stored in a rigid container or box in the refrigerator and wrapped separately.

Bread can be kept in the refrigerator or in a bread bin in a cool cupboard. It is always a good idea to wrap the bread to keep it fresher.

Safety in the Kitchen

Heat Use oven gloves when handling anything that is hot. Never try to take something out of a hot oven without using oven gloves.

▌When using saucepans, hot dishes or baking tins, use both hands and check first that there is nothing in the way of where you are going to place them once you have removed them from the hob or the oven.

▌Place hot pans and dishes on a trivet or board. If you feel that a pan or dish is too heavy for you to handle, then ask someone to do it for you.

▌When on the hob, keep pan handles turned away from you. Angle them to the side and not over the cooker rings which, if turned on, will heat the handles making them too hot to handle.

▌Do not overfill saucepans as they will then be too heavy to lift. There is also the danger that the contents may boil over if the pan is filled close to the brim.

▌Call an adult immediately if a fire breaks out. Do NOT try to deal with it yourself.

▌Do not be tempted to test for heat by placing your hand or fingers on or in anything that may be hot.

▌Turn off the cooker, microwave and any electrical implements that have been used as soon as you have finished with them.

▌As well as informing an adult when you are beginning to cook you must also tell them when you have finished so they can check that electrical implements are safely turned off.

CHAPTER ONE

A Pocket Full of Goodness

Tex Mex Pittas

SERVES 2 (Makes 4 pitta halves)

YOU WILL NEED

2 wholemeal or white pitta breads

3–4 crisp lettuce leaves, such as iceberg

½ small red pepper

2.5cm (1in) piece cucumber

100g (4oz) cooked chicken

25g (1oz) sweetcorn kernels

2 tablespoons tomato and chilli relish

1 **Pre-heat the oven to 180°C/ 350°F/Gas Mark 4. Warm the pitta breads by placing in the oven for 1–2 minutes. Transfer to a chopping board and, with a sharp knife, cut the pittas in half across the middle.** Open them to form pockets.

2 Rinse the lettuce in cold water and pat dry then **shred into thin strips** on the board. Place the lettuce inside the pittas, pushing it down to the base.

3 **Carefully take out the seeds and the white membrane from the pepper by cutting out the stalk then slicing it in two lengthwise.** Rinse and pat dry. **Cut into thin strips**.

Peel the cucumber and **slice thinly** on the chopping board.

4 Wash the chopping board and knife or use clean ones. Remove any skin from the chicken. Place it on the chopping board and **cut into thin strips.**

5 Holding one pitta pocket in your hand, put a few strips of pepper, some cucumber slices and chicken strips on top of the shredded lettuce.

Spoon in a quarter of the sweetcorn then wrap in clear wrap. Fill the other pitta halves with the remaining ingredients then put two in a lunch box.

6 Spoon a little of the relish into a small tub with a lid and add to the lunch box along with two Yankee Doodle Squares (see page 76).

Mini Indian Bites

SERVES 2 (Makes 8)

YOU WILL NEED

8 mini pittas
3 tablespoons mayonnaise
1–2 teaspoons curry powder
25g (1oz) sultanas
1 celery stick
90g (3½oz) can tuna in oil

1 **To warm the pittas either place them in an oven pre-heated to 180°C/350°F/Gas Mark 4 for 2–3 minutes or place in the toaster for 1–2 minutes.**

Transfer to a chopping board taking care not to burn your fingers and, with a sharp knife, cut a slit in the top of each pitta to form pockets.

2 Place the mayonnaise in a bowl and stir in the curry powder. Mix until all the curry powder has been absorbed.

3 Stir the sultanas into the mayonnaise.

4 **Cut off the top and bottom of the celery** then rinse under the tap. Place on the board and **chop into small pieces.** Stir into the mayonnaise.

5 **Open the can of tuna** and place the contents into a sieve. Stir lightly to allow the oil to be drained off then place the drained tuna in a clean bowl and flake into small pieces using a fork.

6 Stir the tuna into the mayonnaise then mix all the ingredients lightly together.

7 Spoon the filling into the split pittas.

8 Serve the pittas on a plate garnished with lettuce or wrap in clear film or foil and place in a lunch box.

Tacos with Potato Salad

SERVES 4

YOU WILL NEED

225g (8oz) new potatoes

salt and pepper

2 celery sticks

1 small red apple

juice ½ lemon

50g (2oz) walnuts

1 tablespoon freshly chopped mint

3 tablespoons mayonnaise or
   fromage frais

4 taco shells

2–3 crisp lettuce leaves

2 tablespoons canned refried beans

50g (2oz) Cheddar cheese, grated

1 **Pre-heat the oven to 180°C/ 350°F/Gas Mark 4.** Scrub or scrape the potatoes and, if large, **cut in half or quarters.** Place in a pan and cover with cold water. Add a pinch of salt. **Place on the hob and bring to the boil, then reduce the heat and cover with a lid. Simmer for 15 minutes or until the potatoes are tender when pierced with a round bladed knife or fork.**

Remove the pan from the heat and drain the potatoes through a colander and place in a bowl.

Trim the celery and wash well then place on a chopping board and carefully **cut into small pieces.** Add to the cooked, drained potatoes.

2 Wash and dry the apple, **cut into quarters then remove the core. Chop the apple into small chunks.** Place the lemon juice in a small bowl then add the apple and turn the apple pieces in the juice until coated. Drain and add to the potatoes.

3 **Lightly chop the walnuts in a cup with a pair of scissors** and add to the potatoes with the chopped mint.

4 Add a little salt and pepper, then the mayonnaise or fromage frais. Stir lightly until evenly coated.

5 Place the taco shells upside down on a baking sheet and **warm in the oven for about 2 minutes. Remove and leave to cool before using.**
   Lightly rinse the lettuce in a colander, drain and **shred into thin strips**. Place the refried beans in a small bowl and mash until smooth.

6 Place the lettuce in the bottom of the taco shells and top with the refried beans. Spoon the potato salad on top then sprinkle the tacos with the grated cheese.

7 Serve on a plate garnished with salad or wrap in clear film or foil and place in a lunch box.

Baby Naans with Winter Salad

SERVES 2 (Makes 4)

YOU WILL NEED

¼ small red cabbage
1 green eating apple
1 tablespoon lemon juice
25g (1oz) sweetcorn kernels,
    canned or cooked from
    frozen
6 radishes, washed
100g (4oz) ham, sliced
25g (1oz) walnuts or pecan nuts
3 tablespoons mayonnaise
4 baby naans

1 **Place the cabbage on a chopping board and cut off the hard central core, any outside damaged leaves and discard. Using a sharp knife, carefully shred the cabbage into thin strips. Cut out the central white core and discard.**

2 Place the cabbage in a large bowl of water and rinse well. Drain in a colander then place in a mixing bowl.

3 **Cut the apple into quarters then cut out and discard the core. Cut into small chunks** and sprinkle with the lemon juice. Add to the cabbage together with the sweetcorn kernels. Mix together.

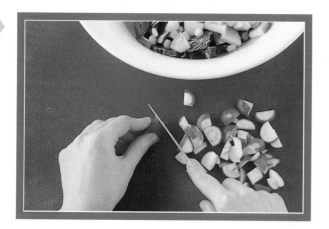

4 **Trim the radishes top and bottom then chop into small pieces.** Add to the bowl.

5 **Cut the ham into small cubes** and stir into the coleslaw.

6 **Chop the walnuts or pecans in a cup with scissors** and add to the cabbage and mix all the ingredients together.

7 Spoon in the mayonnaise then mix lightly together with a spoon until all the ingredients are lightly coated.

8 **Split the naans with a small sharp knife** and gently open up.

9 Fill the naans with the prepared coleslaw.

10 Wrap in foil or clear wrap and place in a lunch box, or serve immediately.

Baked Samosas

SERVES 4 (Makes 8)

YOU WILL NEED

1 tablespoon oil

½ small onion, peeled and chopped

1 small celery stick, trimmed
  and chopped

1 tablespoon red pepper, chopped

1 small carrot, peeled and grated

2 teaspoons mild curry powder

100g (4oz) cooked potato

25g (1oz) frozen peas, thawed

4 sheets filo pastry

50g (2oz) melted butter

1 **Pre-heat the oven to 190°C/375°F/Gas Mark 5. Heat the oil in a frying pan then gently fry the onion and celery for 5 minutes or until softened.**

2 Add the red pepper and carrot and continue to fry for 2 more minutes.

3 Sprinkle in the curry powder and cook gently for 3 minutes, stirring all the time. Remove from the heat.

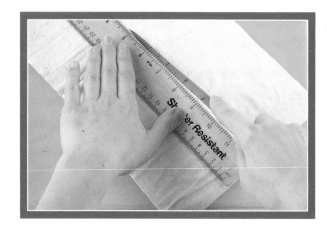

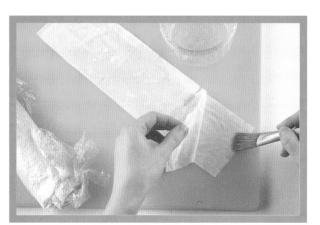

4 **Cut the potato into small cubes** and mix in to the frying pan with the peas.

5 **Cut the filo pastry in half** to form strips about 18cm x 7.5cm (7in x 3in).

6 Brush one strip with a little melted butter and place a second strip on top. (Keep the remaining filo pastry wrapped in clear wrap so that it does not become dry and brittle.)

7 Place a spoonful of the filling in the middle of the strip and at the bottom edge. Brush the edges lightly with a little melted butter.

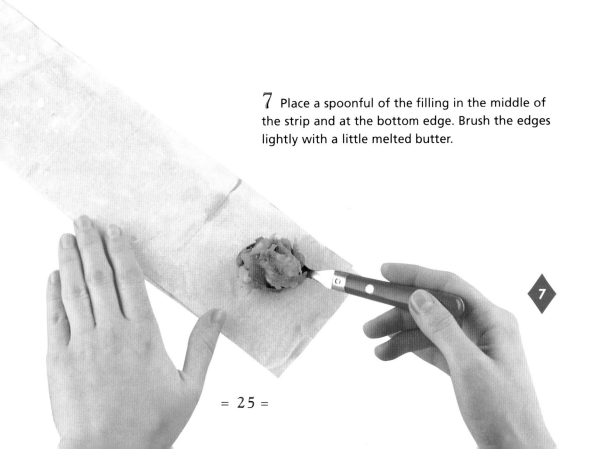

9 Continue to fold the pastry keeping the triangle shape and folding the stuffed portion away from you until the strip of pastry has been used. Repeat until all the pastry and filling has been used.

10 Brush the pastry with butter before you make the final fold, so that the edges stick together while cooking.

11 Place on a lightly-oiled baking sheet, brush with melted butter and **bake for 15 minutes or until crisp.** Cool, then pack into a lunch box or serve hot, warm or cold.

8 Fold the pastry over lengthways to form a triangle.

CHAPTER TWO

Pick a Stick

Aubergine Satay with Tomato Marinade

· ·

SERVES 2–3 (Makes 6)

YOU WILL NEED

FOR THE MARINADE

2 tablespoons tomato purée
2 tablespoons olive oil
4 tablespoons orange juice
1 teaspoon garlic purée
½ teaspoon chilli purée

FOR THE SATAYS

1 aubergine
1 tablespoon sesame seeds
6 small satay sticks

1 For the marinade, in a bowl, mix the tomato purée with the oil, orange juice, garlic and chilli purée until well blended and reserve.

2 **For the satays, trim the ends off the aubergine and slice thinly lengthwise.**

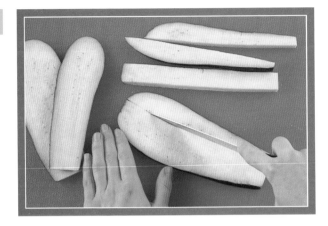

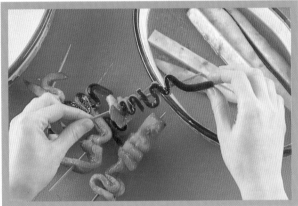

6 **Pre-heat the grill to high.** Line the grill rack with foil and **grill the satays for about 6–8 minutes or until cooked. Turn them occasionally and spoon over a little of the reserved marinade as they cook. Turn down the grill if they start to burn.**

When cooked, remove the satays from the heat and sprinkle with the sesame seeds. Allow to cool before wrapping, ready to put into the lunch box, or serving on a bed of lettuce.

3 **Cut each slice into strips** about 2cm (¾in) wide and place in a shallow dish.

4 Pour the reserved marinade over the aubergine then turn the strips in the marinade. Cover and chill in the refrigerator for at least 1 hour, turning the strips occasionally in the marinade.

Soak the wooden satay sticks in cold water for 30 minutes then drain.

5 Remove the aubergine strips from the dish, allowing the marinade to drain off each one as you take it out, then thread each strip onto the soaked satay stick. Reserve the marinade.

Mini Kebabs with Cheese Dip

SERVES 2–4 (Makes 8)

YOU WILL NEED

FOR THE KEBABS

7.5cm (3in) piece cucumber

4 baby corn

8 cherry tomatoes

100g (4oz) Edam cheese

8 no-need-to-soak prunes
  (optional)

FOR THE DIP

50g (2oz) soft cream cheese

1 tablespoon tomato ketchup

4 spring onions, trimmed and
  finely chopped

salt and pepper

8 small satay sticks or 16
  cocktail sticks

1 For the kebabs, rinse the cucumber and score the skin with the prongs of a fork to give a decorative pattern. **Cut into bite-sized pieces.**
  Cover the baby corn with boiling water, leave for two minutes then drain. When cool enough to handle **cut in half** widthways and reserve.

2 Rinse and pat dry the cherry tomatoes.

3

4

5

6

7

3 Peel off or **cut away the rind from the cheese and discard. Cut the cheese into bite-sized cubes.**

4 Thread the halved baby corn, cucumber, tomatoes, cheese, and prunes (if using) onto cocktail or small satay sticks. Put on a plate and cover with clear wrap.

5 For the dip, beat the cream cheese and tomato ketchup together until soft and smooth.

6 Mix in the chopped spring onions. Add salt and pepper to taste.

7 Place the dip in small containers and cover and place in a lunch box with the kebabs, or serve on a plate surrounded by the mini kebabs.

Chicken Sticks with Cucumber Dip

SERVES 2–3 (Makes 6)

YOU WILL NEED

FOR THE STICKS

100g (4oz) boneless chicken breast

2 tablespoons sunflower or olive oil

4 tablespoons freshly squeezed orange juice

1 tablespoon freshly chopped mint

FOR THE DIP

2.5cm (1in) piece cucumber

1 tablespoon freshly chopped mint

150ml (¼pt) natural fromage frais or natural yogurt

carrot, celery and pepper sticks

6 small satay sticks

1 For the chicken sticks, discard any skin from the chicken and **cut into thin strips** about 6mm x 7.5cm (¼in x 3in). Place in a shallow dish.

2 Mix the oil with the orange juice and mint and spoon over the chicken. Cover and leave in the refrigerator for at least 30 minutes, turning in the marinade occasionally.

Soak the satay sticks in cold water for 30 minutes.

3

4

5

6

3 For the dip, <u>peel the cucumber and</u>
chop into small pieces.

4 Mix the cucumber and mint into the
fromage frais or yogurt. Stir well and place
into a small serving bowl.

5 **Pre-heat the grill** to high and line the
grill rack with foil.
   Remove the chicken strips allowing the
marinade to drain off each one before
threading it onto a soaked satay stick.
Reserve the marinade.

6 **Grill for 8–10 minutes or until**
thoroughly cooked. Turn occasionally and
brush with the marinade. Remove from
the grill and serve with the dip and
vegetable sticks.

Turkey Satay with Peanut Dip

SERVES 2–3 (Makes 6)

YOU WILL NEED

100g (4oz) boneless turkey
   breast
1 red chilli
2 tablespoons smooth peanut
   butter
150ml (¼pt) natural yogurt
juice of 1 lemon
6 small satay sticks

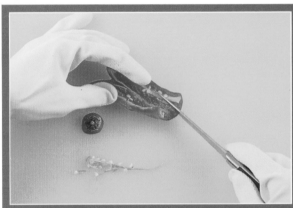

1 Pull off and discard any skin from the turkey
and **cut into thin** strips about 6mm x 7.5cm
(¼in x 3in). Place in a shallow dish.

2 Using rubber gloves, make a **cut down the
length of the chilli** and remove the stalk, all the
seeds and the pithy white membrane from the
inside. Rinse under cold water then chop
finely. (Take care not to touch your face while
handling the chilli and wash the rubber gloves and
your hands thoroughly afterwards.)

3 Place the peanut butter in a small, heavy-based
pan with the chopped chilli and lemon juice.

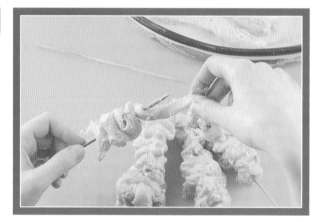

4 **Heat gently,** stirring occasionally with a wooden spoon for about 3–5 minutes or until blended and smooth.

Remove from the heat and slowly stir in the yogurt.

5 Pour half of the mixture over the turkey strips, cover and leave for 30 minutes in the refrigerator. Turn the turkey strips occasionally during this time. Place the rest of the peanut mixture into a small sealable container.

Soak the wooden satay sticks in cold water for 30 minutes then drain. Line the grill rack with foil.

6 **Pre-heat the grill to high.** Remove the turkey strips and allow the marinade to drain off each one before threading it onto a soaked satay stick. Reserve the marinade.

Grill for 8 minutes or until cooked. Turn occasionally and brush with the marinade.

7 When cool, wrap in tin foil or clear wrap and pack into a lunch box with the remaining peanut dip.

Salad Stickers

SERVES 2–4 (Makes 4)

YOU WILL NEED

FOR THE STICKS

4 baby carrots
¼ small red pepper
2 celery sticks
4 spring onions
50g (2oz) Cheddar cheese
8 cherry tomatoes, rinsed
4 wooden satay sticks

FOR THE DIP

2 tablespoons mayonnaise
2 tablespoons houmous

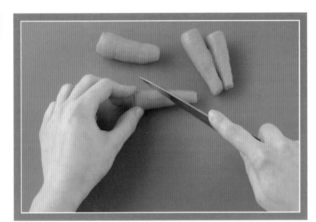

1 For the sticks, scrub the carrots, trim and cut in half if large. **Put in a pan of cold, lightly salted water, bring to the boil then simmer for 2 minutes, drain and allow to cool.**

2 **De-seed the pepper and discard the pithy membrane, then cut into chunky pieces.**

3 **Trim the celery** and wash under cold water **then cut into bite-sized pieces.**

4 **Trim the spring onions then rinse. Cut into bite-sized pieces.**

5 **Cut the cheddar cheese into small cubes.**

6 Rinse the tomatoes and dry on absorbent kitchen paper. Thread all the ingredients onto small wooden satay sticks. Then, either wrap in clear wrap and place in a lunch box or arrange on a plate.

7 For the dip, mix the mayonnaise with the houmous and place in a small sealable container and place in the lunch box, or spoon into a small bowl and serve with the sticks.

CHAPTER THREE

Open Toppers

Curried Chicken Wedge

SERVES 4–8 (Makes 8 slices)

YOU WILL NEED

225g (8oz) prepared shortcrust
   pastry
2 tablespoons oil
1 small onion, peeled and chopped
2 garlic cloves, peeled and crushed
1 tablespoon mild curry powder
300g (10oz) cooked chicken
3 eggs, size 3
150ml (¼pt) single cream or milk
salt and pepper
1 tablespoon freshly chopped
   coriander

1 **Pre-heat the oven to 200°C/400°F/Gas Mark 6.**
Roll the prepared pastry out on a lightly floured surface to a circle about 25.5cm (10in) in diameter.

2 Carefully wrap the pastry round the rolling pin and unroll it over a loose bottomed 20.5cm (8in) fluted flan tin.

3 Gently ease the pastry into edges and base of the flan tin taking care not to tear it. Roll the rolling pin over the top to achieve a neat edge. Chill in the refrigerator for 30 minutes.

4 Place a sheet of crumpled tin foil or greaseproof paper and baking beans into the base of the pastry case to stop the pastry rising. Bake for 15 minutes. **Remove from the oven and discard the foil or paper and beans.**

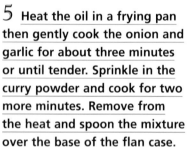

5 **Heat the oil in a frying pan then gently cook the onion and garlic for about three minutes or until tender. Sprinkle in the curry powder and cook for two more minutes. Remove from the heat and spoon the mixture over the base of the flan case.**

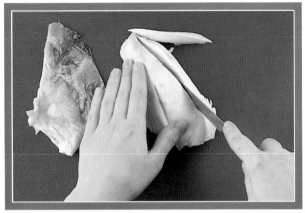

6 Remove any skin or bone from the chicken and **cut into thin strips.** Scatter over the onion mixture.

7 Beat together the eggs, cream or milk, seasoning and coriander then pour over the chicken mixture.

8 **Return the flan to the oven** and cook for 15 minutes **then lower the oven temperature to 180°C, 350°F, Gas Mark 4** and continue to cook for a further 20–30 minutes or until set. **Remove from the oven** and cool before cutting into wedges and serving.

Topping Pizza

SERVES 2 (Makes 2)

YOU WILL NEED

1 small green pepper
3 tomatoes
50g (2oz) mushrooms
1 small onion
1 tablespoon oil
2 tablespoons tomato purée
2 individual 14cm (5in) pizza
   bases
50g (20z) Cheddar or
   mozzarella cheese, grated

1 **Pre-heat the oven to 220°C/425°F/Gas Mark 7** and lightly oil a baking sheet.

   Cut the top of the pepper and discard the seeds and pithy membrane, rinse, **then slice into thin strips.**

2 **Make a small cross in the top of the tomatoes, place in a large bowl and carefully cover with boiling water. Leave for 2 minutes then drain. When cool enough to handle, peel off the skin. Place on a chopping board and chop into small pieces.**

3 Wipe the mushrooms with absorbent kitchen paper and **slice thinly.**

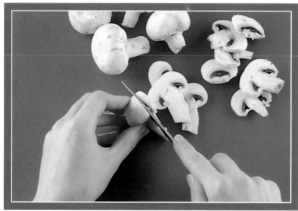

4 **Using a small sharp knife peel and chop the onion. Heat the oil in a frying pan and gently cook the onion for 3 minutes, stirring occasionally.**

5 Add the pepper to the onion and cook for 2 more minutes. **Add the chopped tomatoes and mushrooms and cook for 3 more minutes.**

6 Blend the tomato purée with 2 tablespoons of water and **stir into the pan, then cook for a further 3 minutes.**

7 Spoon the prepared filling over the pizza bases and sprinkle with the cheese.

8 **Bake in the pre-heated oven** for 12–15 minutes or until the cheese has melted and is brown and bubbly. **Remove from the oven** and cool completely before wrapping or serve hot, straight from the oven.

Mini Tuna Tartlets

SERVES 4 (Makes 4)

YOU WILL NEED

175g (6oz) prepared shortcrust
   pastry
200g (7oz) can tuna
3 tablespoons mayonnaise
grated rind of 1 small lemon
2 celery sticks, trimmed and
   finely chopped
5 spring onions, trimmed and
   chopped
parsley or coriander sprigs, to
   garnish

1 **Pre-heat the oven to 200°C/400°F/Gas Mark 6.**
   Roll the pastry out on a lightly floured surface
and use to line four 10cm (4in) individual flan tins.

2 Prick the bases lightly with a fork and allow to
relax in the fridge for 30 minutes.

3 Place a sheet of crumpled tin foil or
greaseproof paper and baking beans in the bases
of the flan tins then **bake in the oven for 15
minutes. Take out of the oven and remove the tin
foil or the paper and beans.** Leave to cool before
filling.

4 Drain the tuna, place in a bowl and flake into small pieces with a fork.

5 Add the mayonnaise to the tuna together with the lemon rind, chopped celery and 4 of the spring onions, and mix the ingredients together.

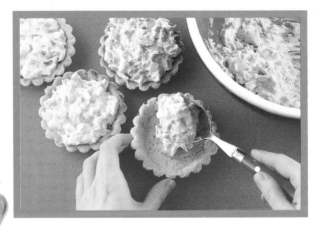

6 Pile the mixture into the cooked flan cases and sprinkle with the remaining spring onion.

7 Either wrap in clear wrap or foil before placing in the lunch box or served garnished with coriander or parsley.

Pizza Swirls

SERVES 3–4 (Makes 6–8 slices)

YOU WILL NEED

FOR THE PIZZA BASE

225g (8oz) self-raising flour
pinch salt
½ teaspoon mustard
  powder
50g (2oz) butter or
  margarine
50g (2oz) Cheddar
  cheese, grated
6–8 tablespoons milk

FOR THE FILLING

2 tablespoons tomato purée
1 small onion, peeled and
  grated
1 red pepper, de-seeded and
  finely chopped
100g (4oz) ham, finely chopped
1 tablespoon freshly chopped
  parsley
50g (2oz) Cheddar cheese,
  grated

1 **Pre-heat the oven to 220°C/425°F/Gas Mark 7** and lightly oil a baking sheet.
   For the pizza bases, place the flour, salt and mustard into a dry sieve and sift into large bowl.

2 **Cut the butter or margarine into small pieces** and add to the flour. With your fingertips, rub the butter or margarine into the flour, until the mixture resembles fine breadcrumbs. Stir in the cheese.
   Slowly add the milk and mix to form a soft, but not sticky, dough. Add a little extra milk if necessary. Knead until the dough is smooth and pliable.

3 Roll the dough out on a lightly floured surface to an oblong of about 20.5cm x 25.5cm (8in x 10in).

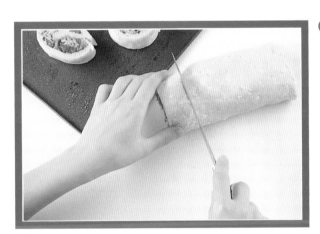

4 For the filling, blend together the tomato purée and 2 tablespoons of water until smooth then stir in the grated onion, chopped pepper, the ham and chopped parsley.

5 Spread the filling over the dough, leaving a gap of about 2.5cm (1in) around the edges. Sprinkle with the grated cheese.

6 Brush the edges lightly with a little water. Roll up from the long end sealing the filling inside the roll.

7 **Cut into 4cm (1½in) slices** and place on the lightly oiled baking sheet.

8 **Bake in the oven for 12–15 minutes or until golden. Remove from the oven** and cool before wrapping and placing in lunch box or serving, garnished and arranged on a plate.

Vegetable Bites

SERVES 4

YOU WILL NEED

FOR THE VEGETABLES

2 celery sticks
½ small cucumber
1 small yellow pepper
1 small red pepper

FOR THE FILLING

4 tablespoons smoked mackerel
   pâté
1 tablespoon natural yogurt
grated rind of ½ a lemon
small bunch of chives
4 satay sticks (optional)

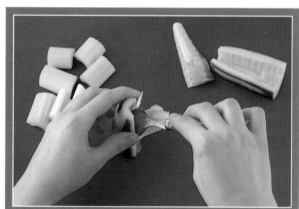

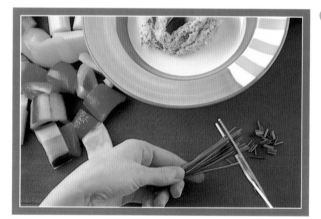

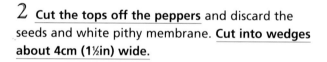

2 **Cut the tops off the peppers** and discard the seeds and white pithy membrane. **Cut into wedges about 4cm (1½in) wide.**

3 Place the smoked mackerel pâté in a bowl then beat in the yogurt and grated lemon rind. Snip the chives into small pieces and add to the filling. Beat all the ingredients together until smooth and creamy. Spoon the filling into the prepared vegetables. Secure on satay sticks for ease of carrying if you wish.

1 Trim and rinse the celery and **cut into 5cm (2in) lengths. Cut the cucumber in half lengthwise and scoop out the seeds and discard. Cut the cucumber into 5cm (2in) pieces.**

CHAPTER FOUR

Sandwiches To Go

Burger and Cheese Dinosaurs

SERVES 4 (Makes 1 dinosaur)

YOU WILL NEED

4 beefburgers
2 teaspoons oil
1 thick French stick
1 tablespoon butter (optional)
few crisp lettuce leaves
4 single cheese slices
2 large tomatoes, sliced
tomato relish or mayonnaise to
    serve

1 **Pre-heat grill to high** and line the grill rack with tin foil. Place the beefburgers on the grill rack. Brush with the oil.

2 **Cook under the grill for 5–8 minutes, turning at least once, or until cooked.** Drain on absorbent kitchen paper and **cut in half.**

3 **Place the French stick on a chopping board and make a long vertical cut along the top of the loaf.** Carefully open up and spread with butter if using.

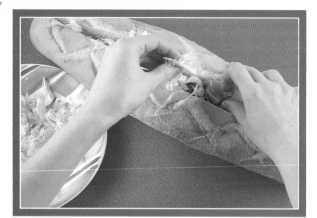

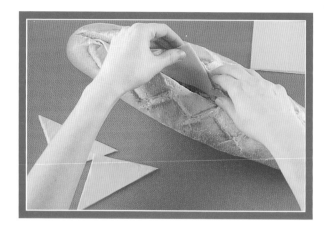

4 Lightly rinse the lettuce and pat dry with absorbent kitchen paper. **Shred the lettuce into thin strips** and place in the base of the loaf.

5 **Cut the cheese slices diagonally in half** and place in the loaf resting on the lettuce, to represent the fins.

6 Arrange the sliced tomatoes and halved beefburgers in the loaf. Press both sides of the French stick lightly together.

7 **Cut into wedges** and serve with either tomato relish or mayonnaise.

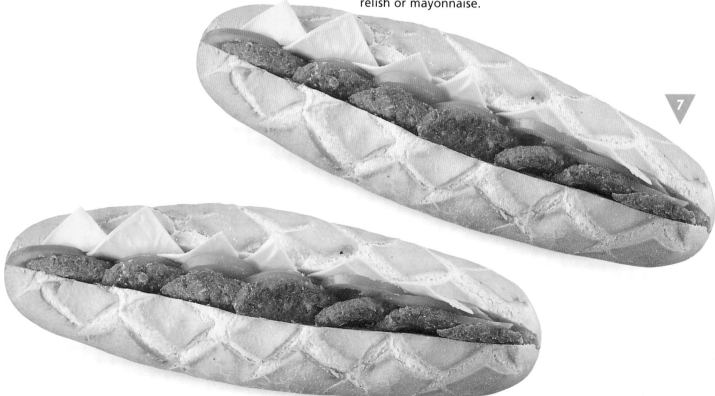

BLT

· · · · · · · · ·

SERVES 1

YOU WILL NEED

2–3 rashers back bacon
3 slices white or wholemeal bread
2 teaspoons softened butter or margarine
2–3 crisp lettuce leaves, such as iceberg
½ large tomato
1 tablespoon mayonnaise
6 thin slices cucumber

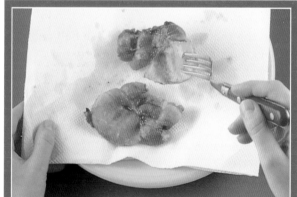

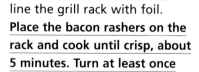

1 **Pre-heat the grill to high** and line the grill rack with foil. **Place the bacon rashers on the rack and cook until crisp, about 5 minutes. Turn at least once** **during this time. Drain on absorbent kitchen paper.**

2 Spread the bread with the butter or margarine.

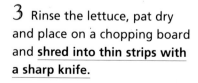

3 Rinse the lettuce, pat dry and place on a chopping board and **shred into thin strips with a sharp knife.**

4 Slice the tomato thinly.

5 Place one slice of bread buttered side up and arrange the cooked bacon rashers on top. Cover with half the shredded lettuce and spoon over a little of the mayonnaise.

6 Top with a second slice of bread, buttered side uppermost and press down lightly.

7 Cover the bread with the rest of the mayonnaise and arrange the remaining lettuce, sliced tomato and cucumber over the top.

8 Finish with the remaining slice of bread, buttered side down and press lightly together. **Cut in half.**

9 Wrap before placing in the lunch box or serve immediately.

Club

. . . .

SERVES 1

YOU WILL NEED

3 slices of granary or white bread

2 teaspoons softened butter or margarine

75g (3oz) cooked chicken

1 tablespoon cranberry sauce or
   mayonnaise

2–3 crisp lettuce leaves, such as cos lettuce

1 tomato

½ small onion, peeled

1 Spread the bread with the butter or margarine. **Cut the chicken into thin slices.**

2 Place one slice of bread, buttered side uppermost, on a board and arrange the sliced chicken on top.

3 Spread with half the cranberry sauce or mayonnaise.

4 Rinse the lettuce and pat dry. **Shred into thin strips** and place half over the chicken. Cover with a slice of bread buttered side up.

5 **Slice the tomato and onion** and place on top of the bread.

6 Dot with the rest of the cranberry sauce or mayonnaise and cover with the remaining shredded lettuce.

7 Cover with the last slice of bread buttered side down and press the sandwich lightly together.

8 **Cut in half** and serve or wrap before placing in the lunch box.

Ham and Coleslaw Double Decker

SERVES 1

YOU WILL NEED

3 slices of granary or white bread
2 teaspoons softened butter or margarine
2 slices of ham
2 teaspoons mango chutney
2 crisp lettuce leaves such as iceberg
2 tablespoons Coleslaw

2 Lightly rinse the lettuce and pat dry with absorbent kitchen paper. **Shred the lettuce with a small sharp knife** and place on top of the chutney and cover with a further slice of bread, buttered side uppermost.

3 Place the coleslaw on top of the bread then cover with the remaining slice of bread, buttered side down. Press together lightly.

4 **Cut in half** and serve with Cheesey Picks (see page 71).

1 Spread the bread with the softened butter or margarine and place one slice on a chopping board, buttered side uppermost. Cover with the ham then spread with the chutney.

King-Size Bap

SERVES 2

YOU WILL NEED

100g (4oz) sausagemeat

2 spring onions

½ small cooking apple

2–3 sprigs fresh mint

salt and pepper

1–2 teaspoons flour

2 baps

2 crisp lettuce leaves, shredded

2 teaspoons mango chutney

2 canned pineapple rings,
   drained

1 **Pre-heat the oven to 200°C/400°F/Gas Mark 6.**
Place the sausagemeat in a bowl and break up
with a fork.

2 **Cut off and discard the root and most of the
green part from the spring onions and chop finely.**
Add to the sausagemeat in the bowl.

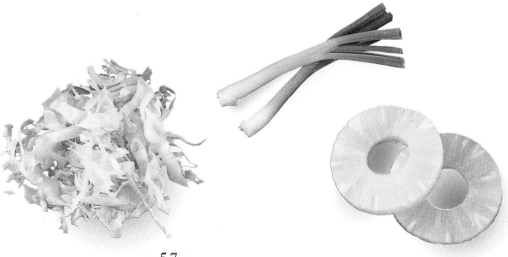

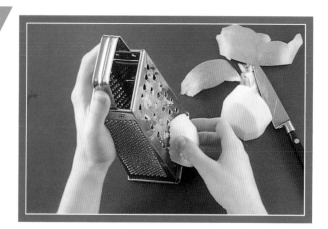

3 **Core the apple and peel, if preferred. Grate on the coarse side of the grater and add to the sausagemeat.**

4 Place the mint in a cup and **chop with a pair of kitchen scissors.** Add to the bowl and season the mixture with salt and pepper.

5 Mix the ingredients together with clean hands then form into two round burger shapes.

6 Coat with the flour, place on a baking sheet and **bake in the oven for 15–20 minutes or until cooked and lightly golden in colour. Remove from the oven.**

7 **Split the baps** (you can lightly toast the baps if you wish) and cover the bases with the lettuce.

8 Place the sausagemeat burgers on top. Dot with the mango chutney.

9 Top with the pineapple ring then cover with the bap lid.

10 Wrap when cool to place in a lunch box or serve immediately, while still warm.

CHAPTER FIVE
Mouthwatering Salads

Rice as Nice

SERVES 4–6

YOU WILL NEED

FOR THE SALAD

100g (4oz) long-grain rice

50g (2oz) frozen sweetcorn

50g (2oz) frozen peas

220g (8oz) can red kidney
    beans or mixed pulses

75g (3oz) cherry tomatoes

FOR THE DRESSING

3 tablespoons olive oil

1 tablespoon lemon juice

1 teaspoon sugar

a pinch of mustard powder

1 tablespoon freshly
    chopped coriander

salt and pepper

1 For the salad, place the rice in a saucepan and cover with cold, lightly salted water. **Bring to the boil then reduce the heat and simmer** for 12–15 minutes or until the rice is tender but not soft.

2 **Drain the rice through a colander** and place in a large mixing bowl.

3 **Cook the sweetcorn and peas together in a pan of gently boiling water** for 3–5 minutes, or until tender.

4 **Drain** and add to the rice.

5 Pour the can of red kidney beans or mixed pulses into a colander and rinse under cold running water. Add to the rice and mix lightly.

6 **Rinse the tomatoes and cut them in half**, then add to the rice and mix again until all the ingredients are evenly distributed.

7 For the dressing, place all the remaining ingredients in a screw-top jar and shake vigorously until they are well blended.

8 Pour over the rice salad and toss lightly.

9 Serve immediately or cover and store for up to 8 hours in the fridge.

Chicken and Pasta Salad

SERVES 4–6

YOU WILL NEED

175g (6oz) boneless chicken breasts

2 tablespoons hoisin sauce

4 tablespoons orange juice

75g (3oz) dried pasta shapes

1 teaspoon sunflower oil

50g (2oz) seedless green grapes

50g (2oz) cherry tomatoes

4 spring onions

7.5cm (3in) piece cucumber

2 tablespoons olive oil

salt and pepper

1 tablespoon freshly chopped coriander

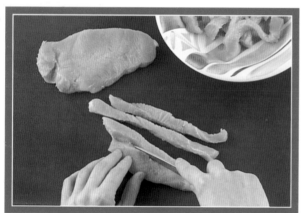

1 Discard any skin from the chicken and **cut into thin strips**, place in a shallow dish. In a pan, **warm the hoisin sauce** then mix with half the orange juice. Pour over the chicken, cover and leave in the refrigerator for 30 minutes. Spoon the marinade over the chicken occasionally during this time.

2 **Bring a medium-sized pan of salted water to the boil and add a little drop of oil. Cook the pasta for 8–10 minutes. Drain and place in a bowl.**

3 Drain the chicken, discarding the marinade, and **heat the remaining oil in a frying pan. Stir fry the chicken for 5–6 minutes. Remove from the pan with a slotted spoon and add to the cooked pasta.**

4 Wipe or rinse the grapes and tomatoes. If large, **cut the tomatoes in half**, then add to the bowl.

5 **Trim the spring onions by cutting off the root, some of the tough green tops and removing any rough outer skin. Place on a chopping board and chop**, then add to the pasta and chicken mixture.

6 **Wash, or peel the cucumber if preferred, then chop it into small pieces.** Add to the bowl and mix all the salad ingredients lightly together.

7 Mix the remaining orange juice, olive oil, salt and pepper and the chopped coriander together and pour over the salad.

8 Toss lightly together then place in a container. Serve immediately or cover and store in the refrigerator for up to 1 day.

Sputniks and Beans

SERVES 3–4 (Makes 8 sputniks)

YOU WILL NEED

225g (8oz) minced lamb
1 small onion
1 tablespoon pine kernels, chopped
grated rind ½ lemon
50g (2oz) fresh white breadcrumbs
1 tablespoon freshly chopped mint
salt and pepper
1 egg yolk (size 5)
25g (1oz) blanched almonds
220g (8oz) can red kidney beans
½ small red pepper
4 spring onions
1 celery stick
2 tomatoes
2–3 tablespoons tomato ketchup

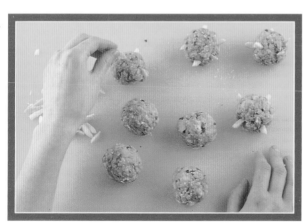

1 **Pre-heat the oven to 190°C/ 375°F/Gas Mark 5.**
Place the lamb in a mixing bowl and break up the lumps with a fork.

2 **Peel the onion, leaving the root on and grate on the coarse side of the grater.** Add to the lamb with the pine kernels, grated lemon rind, breadcrumbs, chopped mint and salt and pepper to taste.

3 Stir the ingredients together then add the egg yolk and mix thoroughly with your hands.
Shape the mixture into small balls and place in a small, lightly oiled roasting tin. **Cut the almonds into two or three to make short "sticks"** and use to stud the meatballs. Cook in the oven for 15–20 minutes or until cooked.

4

5

6

7

4 **Remove from the oven** and drain on absorbent kitchen paper.

5 Drain and rinse the beans in a colander or sieve and place in a small mixing bowl.

6 **De-seed and chop the pepper into small pieces. Trim off the root and the tough green part from the spring onions, removing any tough outer skins and chop finely.** Add to the beans.

7 **Trim the celery and chop into small pieces. Chop the tomatoes** then add them with the spring onions to the beans along with the tomato ketchup.

8 Mix together and serve with the meatball sputniks.

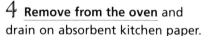

Turk's Veil

SERVES 4–6

YOU WILL NEED
FOR THE SALAD

100g (4oz) couscous

75g (3oz) frozen mixed
vegetables

1 tablespoon freshly
chopped mint

1 tablespoon freshly
chopped parsley

50g (2oz) raisins

50g (2oz) baby button
mushrooms

FOR THE DRESSING

4 tablespoons olive oil

2 tablespoons orange juice

a pinch of dry mustard
powder

1 teaspoon clear honey

1 teaspoon ground
cinnamon

salt and pepper

1 For the salad, place the couscous in a large bowl and **cover with boiling water.** Cover with a clean cloth and leave to stand for 5 minutes or until all the water has been absorbed.

2 Spoon the couscous into a sieve and **place on top of a pan of gently simmering water.** The bottom of the sieve should not touch the water.

3 **Steam for about 5–8 minutes, forking the couscous occasionally to separate the grains. Remove from the heat and place in a bowl.**

4 **Bring a fresh pan of lightly salted water to the boil and add the frozen vegetables. Bring back to the boil and cook for 3–5 minutes.**

5 **Drain and add to the cooked couscous.** Add the chopped herbs with the raisins and mix all the ingredients lightly together.

6 Wipe the mushrooms with absorbent kitchen paper, then slice. Add to the couscous.

7 For the dressing, place all the remaining ingredients in a screw top jar and shake vigorously until well blended.

8 Pour the dressing over the couscous, toss lightly and serve.

CHAPTER SIX

Crunchy Bites

· ·

Cheesey Picks

MAKES about 40

YOU WILL NEED

100g (4oz) plain white flour
½ teaspoon mustard powder
a drop of Tabasco
50g (2oz) butter or margarine
50g (2oz) mature Cheddar
   cheese
1 tablespoon sesame seeds

1 **Pre-heat the oven to 200°C/ 400°F/Gas Mark 6** and lightly oil a baking sheet. Sift the flour, mustard powder and Tabasco into a mixing bowl.

2 Add the butter or margarine to the flour.

3 Using your fingertips, rub in the fat until the mixture resembles fine breadcrumbs.

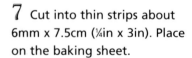

4 **Grate the cheese using the coarse side of the grater,** then stir into the flour and butter or margarine mixture.

5 Using your hands, mix to form a smooth but not sticky dough, adding about 1 teaspoon of cold water to help bring the mixture together.

6 Knead lightly until smooth then roll out on a lightly floured surface to form an oblong about 6mm (¼in) thick.

7 Cut into thin strips about 6mm x 7.5cm (¼in x 3in). Place on the baking sheet.

8 Lightly brush with a little water and sprinkle with the sesame seeds. **Bake in the oven for 12–15 minutes or until golden brown.**

9 Allow to cool before removing from the baking sheet. Arrange on a plate and serve or store in an airtight container for up to 3 days.

Oaty Chews

MAKES 8 slices

YOU WILL NEED

100g (4oz) softened butter or
   margarine
50g (2oz) demerara sugar
3 tablespoons golden syrup
175g (6oz) porridge oats
50g (2oz) chocolate cooking
   chips

1 **Pre-heat the oven to 200°C/
400°F/Gas Mark 6** and lightly oil
a square 18m (7in) tin.

2 Cream the butter or
margarine and sugar together
until pale and soft.

3 Brush a tablespoon with a
little oil then use it to measure
out the syrup. The oil will stop
the syrup sticking to the spoon.
**Warm the syrup in a small
saucepan** then add to the
creamed mixture and beat in.

4 Add the oats and stir with a wooden spoon until they have been thoroughly mixed in.

5 Stir the chocolate cooking chips into the mixture.

6 Turn the mixture into the prepared tin and smooth the top with a palette knife. **Bake in the oven for 20 minutes or until pale golden.**

7 **Remove from the oven and, using a round bladed knife, mark into bars.** Leave in the tin until completely cold.

8 Serve on a plate or store in an airtight tin for up to a week.

Yankee Doodle Squares

MAKES 9 squares

YOU WILL NEED

175g (6oz) plain white flour

100g (4oz) softened butter or margarine

50g (2oz) caster sugar

3 tablespoons smooth peanut butter

100g (4oz) chocolate cake covering

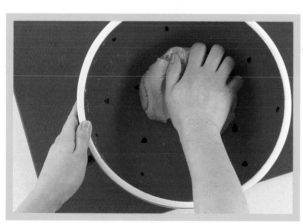

1 **Pre-heat the oven to 180°C/ 350°F/Gas Mark 4** and lightly oil a square 18cm (7in) baking tin.
Sift the flour into a mixing bowl then add the butter or margarine.

2 Rub in the butter or margarine using your fingertips, until the mixture resembles fine breadcrumbs. Stir in the sugar.

3 With your hands, knead the mixture until it comes together and forms a ball in the centre of the bowl.

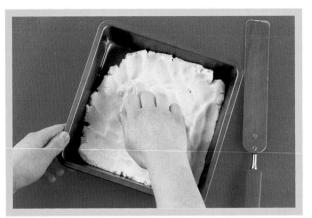

4 Place in the tin and gently pat out the mixture until it fills the base of the tin and is an even thickness.

5 Prick the surface with a fork then **bake in the oven for 20 minutes or until pale golden**.

6 **Remove from the oven** and, using a round bladed knife, gently spread the cooked shortcake with the peanut butter, ensuring that it is evenly coated.

7 **Break the chocolate into small pieces and place in a small bowl standing over a pan of gently simmering water. Stir until melted.**

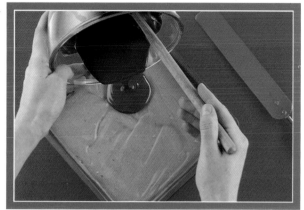

8 **Pour the melted chocolate over the peanut butter.**

9 Spread with a knife until the top is completely covered.

10 Allow the chocolate to set before cutting into squares.

11 Serve or store in an airtight jar for up to a week.

CHAPTER SEVEN

Sweet Delights

Chocolate Crackles

MAKES 8

YOU WILL NEED
100g (4oz) milk chocolate
50g (2oz) butter or margarine
3 tablespoons golden syrup
50g (2oz) cornflakes
25g (1oz) chopped almonds

1 Break the chocolate into small pieces and place in a large, heavy-based saucepan.

2 Add the butter or margarine to the pan.

3 Brush a tablespoon with a little oil then use it to measure the syrup. It will then easily run off the spoon into the pan.
   Place the saucepan over a gentle heat and cook gently, stirring occasionally with a wooden spoon until the ingredients have melted.

4 **Remove from the heat** and stir until the mixture is smooth.

5 Add the cornflakes and nuts and stir with a wooden spoon until they are well coated in the chocolate mixture.

6 Spoon the cornflake crackles into small paper cases.

7 Leave until set before serving. Store in an airtight tin.

Chocolate Fudge Delights

MAKES 8 triangles

YOU WILL NEED

75g (3oz) plain dark chocolate
75g (3oz) butter or margarine
175g (6oz) soft brown sugar
75g (3oz) self-raising flour
2 eggs (size 3)
a few drops of vanilla essence
50g (2oz) flaked almonds
50g (2oz) glacé cherries
1 tablespoon sifted icing sugar

1 **Pre-heat the oven to 180°C/ 350°F/Gas Mark 4** and lightly oil a square 18cm (7in) baking tin. Break the chocolate into small pieces and **place in a pan over a low heat.**

2 **Add the butter or margarine and melt slowly over a gentle heat.** Stir occasionally with a wooden spoon until smooth and free from lumps.

3 **Add the sugar and stir well until thoroughly mixed.**

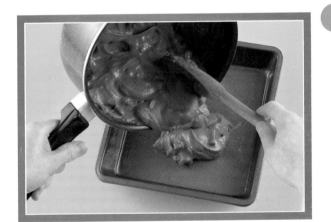

4 **Remove from the heat. Sift the flour into the pan and stir in.**

5 Break the eggs into a bowl and beat. Add to the pan and stir in.

6 Stir in the vanilla essence and flaked almonds.

7 **Chop the cherries on a chopping board** then rinse in warm water and pat dry with absorbent kitchen paper.

8 Stir in the cherries then **spoon the mixture into the prepared tin. Bake in the oven for 30 minutes or until cooked and a skewer inserted into the centre comes out clean.**

9 **Remove from the oven** and mark into four squares.

10 Cut each square in half to form triangles.

11 Leave until cold before removing from the tin and dust with icing sugar.

Apple Crunch

SERVES 2

YOU WILL NEED

450g (1lb) cooking apples
1 teaspoon ground cinnamon
25g (1oz) light soft brown sugar
   or to taste
grated rind ½ lemon
50g (2oz) butter
50g (2oz) fresh white
   breadcrumbs
25g (1oz) almonds, chopped
Mint sprigs, to decorate

1 **Peel the apples and discard the cores. Cut into chunks** and place in a pan with 2 tablespoons of water.

2 **Place the pan over a moderate heat and cook stirring occasionally for 10–12 minutes or until the apples are soft and cooked.**

3 **Remove from the heat** and cool slightly before pouring into a food processor. **Blend to form a purée** then spoon into a small mixing bowl.

4 Stir in the cinnamon, sugar and lemon rind and mix lightly together. Cool and reserve.

5 **Melt the butter in a frying pan then sprinkle in the breadcrumbs. Cook over a gentle heat, stirring frequently for about 5–8 minutes or until the breadcrumbs become crisp and golden.**

6 **Stir in the chopped almonds then remove from the heat.**

7 Layer the apple purée and breadcrumbs in small clear tumblers ending with the breadcrumbs. Serve lukewarm or cold, decorated with a sprig of mint.

8 Cover the tops before packing into a lunch box.

Fruity Sticks

SERVES 4–5 (Makes about 20)

YOU WILL NEED

50g (2oz) seedless green grapes
50g (2oz) seedless red grapes
½ small galia melon
2 satsumas

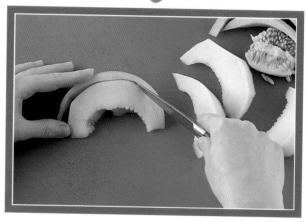

1 Take the grapes off their stalks then rinse in cold water and pat dry with absorbent kitchen paper.

2 Discard the seeds from the melon and **cut off the skin**.

3 **Cut the melon** into small bite sized pieces.

4 Peel the satsumas and take off as much of the white pith as possible.

5 Thread alternate pieces of fruit on to cocktail sticks.

6 Serve on a plate or wrap in clear wrap and place in a lunch box with a small tub of fruit-flavoured fromage frais to use as a dip.

Ready Jelly Go

SERVES 3–4

YOU WILL NEED

1 packet raspberry-flavoured
jelly
1 packet lime-flavoured jelly
1 packet orange-flavoured jelly

1 Place each jelly in a separate jug or bowl and **pour over each one 150ml (¼pt) of boiling water.** Stir until the jellies have melted then add 300ml (½pt) of cold water to each one.

2 Pour a layer of raspberry jelly into 3–4 clear plastic tumblers, place in the fridge and leave until set. (If you want to have the jellies set at a slant, when you put the first layer in the fridge to set, prop the tumblers up at an angle ensuring that the jelly does not tip over while setting. Repeat with the second and third layers.)

3 Cover the first layer of raspberry jelly with a layer of lime jelly and again, place in the fridge until set.

4 Finally pour the orange jelly into the tumblers and leave in the fridge until set.

5 Serve or cover the tops and pack in a lunch box with a small spoon.

Smoothies

SERVES 3–4

YOU WILL NEED
75g (3oz) plain dark chocolate
600ml (1 pint) milk
2 tablespoons cornflour
1 tablespoon sugar
2 teaspoons grated chocolate or
  fresh sliced strawberries, to
  decorate

1 Break the chocolate into small pieces and put into a large pan. Measure out 4 tablespoons from the pint of milk into a separate jug and reserve. **Add the rest of the milk to the pan with the chocolate.**

2 **Place over a gentle heat and allow the chocolate to melt, stirring occasionally.**

3 In a small bowl blend the cornflour to a smooth paste with the reserved 4 tablespoons of milk.

4

5

6

4 **Bring the chocolate milk to the boil then pour in the blended cornflour.**
 Reduce the heat and stir until the mixture thickens. Cook for 1 minute, still stirring.

5 **Remove from the heat** and stir in the sugar.

6 Pour the mixture into small containers. Cool slightly before placing in the refrigerator for at least 4 hours, or until set.

7 Decorate with either a little grated chocolate or sliced strawberries.

7

Strawberry Mousse

SERVES 3

YOU WILL NEED

225g (8oz) ripe strawberries
1 teaspoon gelatine
2 tablespoons orange juice
150ml (¼ pint) Greek-style
    yogurt
1 teaspoon sugar or to taste
3 strawberries, to decorate

1 Rinse the strawberries and pat dry on absorbent kitchen paper.

2 **Place in a food processor and blend to form a purée.** Pass the strawberry purée through a fine sieve, to remove the pips. Place in a bowl.

3 Place the gelatine in a small bowl with the orange juice and **put the bowl over a saucepan of gently simmering water. Heat gently, stirring occasionally with a wooden spoon until the gelatine has dissolved. Cool slightly.**

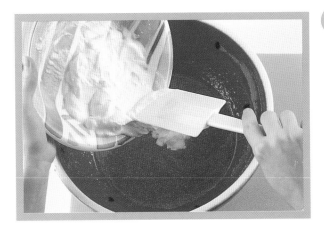

4 Pour the gelatine into the strawberry purée in a thin steady stream and stir continuously.

5 Add the yogurt to the strawberry mixture and stir in gently. Add sugar to taste then pour into small containers.

6 Place in the refrigerator and leave until firm. Cover the tops before packing into a lunch box.

7 Decorate with the strawberries before serving.

Measuring Charts

LIQUID MEASURES

Metric	Imperial
1.25 ml spoon	¼ teaspoons
2.5 ml spoon	½ teaspoon
5 ml spoon	1 teaspoon
15 ml spoon	1 tablespoon
25 ml	1 fl oz
50 ml	2 fl oz
65 ml	2½ fl oz
85 ml	3 fl oz
100 ml	3½ fl oz
120 ml	4 fl oz
135 ml	4½ fl oz
150 ml	¼ pint (5 fl oz) 8 tablespoons
175 ml	6 fl oz
200 ml	7 fl oz (⅓ pint)
250 ml	8 fl oz (1 US cup)
275 ml	9 fl oz
300 ml	½ pint (10 fl oz)
350 ml	12 fl oz
400 ml	14 fl oz
450 ml	¾ pint (15 fl oz)
475 ml	16 fl oz (2 US cups)
500 ml	18 fl oz
600 ml	1 pint (20 fl oz) 2½ US cups
750 ml	1¼ pints
900 ml	1½ pints
1 litre	1¾ pints
1.2 litres	2 pints
1.25 litres	2¼ pints
1.5 litres	2½ pints
1.6 litres	2¾ pints
1.7 litres	3 pints
2 litres	3½ pints
2.25 litres	4 pints
2.5 litres	4½ pints
2.75 litres	5 pints

SOLID MEASURES

Metric	Imperial	Metric	Imperial
10 g	¼ oz	400 g	14 oz
15 g	½ oz	425 g	15 oz
20 g	¾ oz	450 g	1 lb (16 oz)
25 g	1 oz	550 g	1¼ lb
40 g	1½ oz	675 g	1½ lb
50 g	2 oz	900 g	2 lb
65 g	2½ oz	1.25 kg	2½–2¾ lb
75 g	3 oz	1.5 kg	3–3½ lb
90 g	3½ oz	1.75 g	4–4½ lb
100 g	4 oz	2 kg	4½–4¾ lb
120 g	4½ oz	2.25 kg	5–5¼ lb
150 g	5 oz	2.5 kg	5½–5¾ lb
165 g	5½ oz	2.75 kg	6 lb
175 g	6 oz	3 kg	7 lb
185 g	6½ oz	3.5 kg	8 lb
200 g	7 oz	4 kg	9 lb
225 g	8 oz	4.5 kg	10 lb
250 g	9 oz	5 kg	11 lb
300 g	10 oz	5.5 kg	12 lb
325 g	11 oz	6 kg	13 lb
350 g	12 oz	6.5 kg	14 lb
375 g	13 oz	6.75 kg	15 lb

OVEN TEMPERATURES

Centigrade	Fahrenheit	Gas
110°	225°	¼
130°	250°	½
140°	275°	1
150°	300°	2
160°	325°	3
180°	350°	4
190°	375°	5
200°	400°	6
220°	425°	7
230°	450°	8